50 Bartending Recipes for Home

By: Kelly Johnson

Table of Contents

- Martini
- Margarita
- Mojito
- Old Fashioned
- Daiquiri
- Cosmopolitan
- Moscow Mule
- Manhattan
- Whiskey Sour
- Pina Colada
- Negroni
- Mai Tai
- Sangria
- Bloody Mary
- Paloma
- Espresso Martini
- Mint Julep
- Tom Collins
- French 75
- Sidecar
- Blue Lagoon
- White Russian
- Gimlet
- Caipirinha
- Bellini
- Sazerac
- Piña Colada
- Irish Coffee
- Tequila Sunrise
- Aperol Spritz
- Long Island Iced Tea
- Mojito
- Margarita
- Daiquiri
- Manhattan

- Old Fashioned
- Negroni
- Whiskey Sour
- Mai Tai
- Moscow Mule
- Bloody Mary
- Paloma
- Tom Collins
- Mint Julep
- Cosmopolitan
- Piña Colada
- Martini
- Caipirinha
- French 75
- Sangria

Martini

Ingredients:

- 2 oz gin or vodka
- 1/2 oz dry vermouth
- Ice cubes
- Lemon twist or olive for garnish

Instructions:

1. Fill a mixing glass or cocktail shaker with ice cubes.
2. Pour in the gin or vodka and dry vermouth.
3. Stir or shake well (stirring is traditional for a classic Martini) until well chilled.
4. Strain the mixture into a chilled Martini glass.
5. Garnish with a lemon twist or olive.

Enjoy your classic Martini! Adjust the ratio of gin/vodka to vermouth according to your taste preferences—some prefer it drier with less vermouth, while others prefer a more balanced ratio.

Margarita

Ingredients:

- 2 oz tequila (100% agave)
- 1 oz triple sec or Cointreau
- 1 oz fresh lime juice
- 1/2 oz simple syrup (optional, adjust to taste)
- Salt for rimming (optional)
- Lime wheel or wedge for garnish

Instructions:

1. If rimming the glass with salt, moisten the rim with a lime wedge and dip it into salt.
2. Fill a cocktail shaker with ice cubes.
3. Pour in the tequila, triple sec or Cointreau, fresh lime juice, and simple syrup (if using).
4. Shake well until chilled.
5. Strain into a chilled Margarita glass filled with ice (if preferred) or without ice.
6. Garnish with a lime wheel or wedge on the rim of the glass.

Enjoy your classic Margarita! Adjust the sweetness by varying the amount of simple syrup or triple sec according to your preference.

Mojito

Ingredients:

- 2 oz white rum
- 1 oz fresh lime juice
- 1/2 oz simple syrup (adjust to taste)
- 6-8 fresh mint leaves, plus a sprig for garnish
- Club soda
- Ice cubes
- Lime wheel or wedge for garnish

Instructions:

1. In a sturdy glass or cocktail shaker, muddle the mint leaves with the lime juice and simple syrup. Muddling gently releases the mint oils without tearing the leaves.
2. Fill the glass or shaker with ice cubes.
3. Pour in the white rum.
4. Shake well (if using a shaker) or stir thoroughly (if using a glass).
5. Strain the mixture into a highball glass filled with ice cubes.
6. Top with club soda to your preferred level of fizziness.
7. Garnish with a sprig of mint and a lime wheel or wedge on the rim of the glass.

Enjoy your refreshing Mojito! Adjust the sweetness and strength by varying the amount of simple syrup and rum according to your taste preferences.

Old Fashioned

Ingredients:

- 2 oz bourbon or rye whiskey
- 1 sugar cube or 1/2 oz simple syrup
- 2-3 dashes Angostura bitters
- Orange twist or cherry for garnish
- Ice cubes

Instructions:

1. Place the sugar cube in an Old Fashioned glass (or rocks glass).
2. Add 2-3 dashes of Angostura bitters onto the sugar cube.
3. Add a splash of water (optional) to help dissolve the sugar cube. Muddle gently to dissolve the sugar and mix with the bitters.
4. Fill the glass with ice cubes.
5. Pour the bourbon or rye whiskey over the ice.
6. Stir gently to combine the ingredients.
7. Garnish with an orange twist or cherry.

Enjoy your classic Old Fashioned! The simplicity of this cocktail allows the whiskey to shine, balanced with the sweetness from the sugar and depth from the bitters. Adjust the sweetness by varying the amount of sugar or simple syrup to suit your taste.

Daiquiri

Ingredients:

- 2 oz white rum
- 1 oz fresh lime juice
- 1/2 oz simple syrup (adjust to taste)
- Ice cubes

Instructions:

1. Fill a cocktail shaker with ice cubes.
2. Pour in the white rum, fresh lime juice, and simple syrup.
3. Shake well until chilled.
4. Strain into a chilled cocktail glass.
5. Garnish with a lime wheel or wedge.

Enjoy your classic Daiquiri! Adjust the sweetness by varying the amount of simple syrup according to your preference. This cocktail is refreshing and perfect for showcasing the balance of rum, lime juice, and sweetness.

Cosmopolitan

Ingredients:

- 1 1/2 oz vodka
- 1 oz triple sec (Cointreau or any orange liqueur)
- 1/2 oz fresh lime juice
- 1/2 oz cranberry juice
- Ice cubes
- Orange twist or lime wedge for garnish

Instructions:

1. Fill a cocktail shaker with ice cubes.
2. Add vodka, triple sec, fresh lime juice, and cranberry juice to the shaker.
3. Shake well until chilled.
4. Strain into a chilled cocktail glass.
5. Garnish with an orange twist or lime wedge.

Enjoy your classic Cosmopolitan! This cocktail is known for its balance of sweet and tart flavors, making it a popular choice for many occasions. Adjust the sweetness and tartness by varying the amount of cranberry juice and lime juice according to your taste preference.

Moscow Mule

Ingredients:

- 2 oz vodka
- 1/2 oz fresh lime juice
- 4-6 oz ginger beer
- Ice cubes
- Lime wheel or wedge for garnish

Instructions:

1. Fill a copper mug (traditionally used for Moscow Mules) or a highball glass with ice cubes.
2. Pour in the vodka and fresh lime juice.
3. Top off with ginger beer, leaving some room at the top.
4. Stir gently to combine.
5. Garnish with a lime wheel or wedge on the rim of the glass.

Enjoy your refreshing Moscow Mule! The combination of vodka, lime juice, and spicy ginger beer creates a zesty and invigorating cocktail. Adjust the amount of ginger beer to your preferred level of sweetness and spiciness.

Manhattan

Ingredients:

- 2 oz rye whiskey or bourbon
- 1 oz sweet vermouth
- 2 dashes Angostura bitters
- Maraschino cherry for garnish
- Ice cubes

Instructions:

1. Fill a mixing glass or cocktail shaker with ice cubes.
2. Add rye whiskey (or bourbon), sweet vermouth, and Angostura bitters.
3. Stir well until chilled and properly diluted (about 30 seconds if stirring).
4. Strain into a chilled cocktail glass or coupe.
5. Garnish with a maraschino cherry.

Enjoy your classic Manhattan! This cocktail is known for its smooth and balanced flavor profile, combining the richness of whiskey with the sweetness of vermouth and the complexity of bitters. Adjust the proportions of whiskey and vermouth to suit your taste preferences.

Whiskey Sour

Ingredients:

- 2 oz whiskey (bourbon or rye)
- 3/4 oz fresh lemon juice
- 1/2 oz simple syrup
- Ice cubes
- Lemon wheel or cherry for garnish

Instructions:

1. Fill a cocktail shaker with ice cubes.
2. Add whiskey, fresh lemon juice, and simple syrup to the shaker.
3. Shake well until chilled.
4. Strain into a rocks glass filled with ice cubes.
5. Garnish with a lemon wheel or cherry.

Enjoy your classic Whiskey Sour! This cocktail is known for its balanced combination of whiskey's richness, lemon's tartness, and simple syrup's sweetness. Adjust the sweetness by varying the amount of simple syrup according to your taste preference.

Pina Colada

Ingredients:

- 2 oz white rum
- 3 oz pineapple juice
- 1 oz coconut cream
- 1 oz heavy cream (optional, for a creamier texture)
- 1/2 oz simple syrup (optional, adjust to taste)
- Pineapple slice and maraschino cherry for garnish
- Ice cubes

Instructions:

1. In a blender, combine white rum, pineapple juice, coconut cream, heavy cream (if using), and simple syrup (if using).
2. Add a handful of ice cubes.
3. Blend until smooth and creamy.
4. Pour into a chilled hurricane glass or any tall glass.
5. Garnish with a pineapple slice and maraschino cherry.

Enjoy your classic Pina Colada! This tropical cocktail is known for its creamy coconut and sweet pineapple flavors, perfect for relaxing by the beach or poolside. Adjust the sweetness and creaminess according to your taste preferences.

Negroni

Ingredients:

- 1 oz gin
- 1 oz Campari
- 1 oz sweet vermouth
- Orange twist or slice for garnish
- Ice cubes

Instructions:

1. Fill a mixing glass or cocktail shaker with ice cubes.
2. Add gin, Campari, and sweet vermouth to the shaker.
3. Stir well until chilled and properly diluted (about 30 seconds if stirring).
4. Strain into a rocks glass filled with ice cubes.
5. Garnish with an orange twist or slice.

Enjoy your classic Negroni! This cocktail is known for its bold and bitter flavors, balanced with the sweetness of vermouth and the herbal notes of Campari. Adjust the proportions slightly to suit your taste preferences, especially if you prefer it more or less bitter.

Mai Tai

Ingredients:

- 2 oz aged rum
- 3/4 oz orange curaçao or triple sec
- 1/2 oz Orgeat syrup
- 1/2 oz fresh lime juice
- 1/4 oz simple syrup (optional, adjust to taste)
- Mint sprig and lime wheel for garnish
- Crushed ice

Instructions:

1. Fill a cocktail shaker with crushed ice.
2. Add aged rum, orange curaçao or triple sec, Orgeat syrup, fresh lime juice, and simple syrup (if using).
3. Shake well until chilled.
4. Strain into a rocks glass filled with crushed ice.
5. Garnish with a mint sprig and lime wheel.

Enjoy your classic Mai Tai! This cocktail is known for its tropical flavors and balanced sweetness, with hints of almond from the Orgeat syrup. Adjust the sweetness by varying the amount of simple syrup according to your taste preference.

Sangria

Ingredients:

- 1 bottle (750 ml) red wine (Spanish red wine like Rioja or Tempranillo works well)
- 1/4 cup brandy or orange liqueur (e.g., Triple Sec)
- 1/4 cup orange juice
- 1/4 cup simple syrup (adjust to taste)
- 1 orange, sliced
- 1 lemon, sliced
- 1 lime, sliced
- 1 apple, cored and sliced
- 1 cup fresh berries (e.g., strawberries, raspberries, blueberries)
- 1-2 cups club soda or lemon-lime soda (optional, for fizz)

Instructions:

1. In a large pitcher or punch bowl, combine the red wine, brandy or orange liqueur, orange juice, and simple syrup.
2. Stir well to mix.
3. Add the sliced orange, lemon, lime, apple, and berries to the pitcher.
4. Refrigerate for at least 2-4 hours, or preferably overnight, to allow the flavors to meld together.
5. Before serving, add club soda or lemon-lime soda if you prefer a bubbly Sangria.
6. Serve over ice in glasses, ensuring each serving has some fruit.

Enjoy your refreshing and fruity Sangria! Adjust the sweetness with more or less simple syrup according to your taste. It's perfect for gatherings and parties, especially during warm weather.

Bloody Mary

Ingredients:

- 1 1/2 oz vodka
- 3 oz tomato juice
- 1/2 oz fresh lemon juice
- 2 dashes Worcestershire sauce
- 2 dashes hot sauce (e.g., Tabasco)
- Pinch of salt and pepper
- Celery salt (optional, for rimming)
- Celery stalk, lemon wedge, and/or olive for garnish
- Ice cubes

Instructions:

1. If rimming the glass with celery salt, moisten the rim with a lemon wedge and dip it into celery salt.
2. Fill a tall glass (Collins glass) or a large cocktail shaker with ice cubes.
3. Add vodka, tomato juice, fresh lemon juice, Worcestershire sauce, hot sauce, salt, and pepper to the glass or shaker.
4. Stir well to mix all ingredients.
5. Garnish with a celery stalk, lemon wedge, and/or olive.

Enjoy your classic Bloody Mary! Adjust the spiciness and seasoning to your taste preferences by varying the amount of hot sauce and Worcestershire sauce. It's a perfect brunch cocktail, known for its savory and tangy flavors.

Paloma

Ingredients:

- 2 oz tequila (preferably blanco or reposado)
- 1/2 oz fresh lime juice
- 4 oz grapefruit soda (such as Jarritos or Squirt)
- Salt for rimming (optional)
- Lime wedge or grapefruit slice for garnish
- Ice cubes

Instructions:

1. If rimming the glass with salt, moisten the rim with a lime wedge and dip it into salt.
2. Fill a tall glass (Collins glass) or a large cocktail shaker with ice cubes.
3. Pour in the tequila and fresh lime juice.
4. Stir briefly to mix.
5. Top with grapefruit soda.
6. Garnish with a lime wedge or grapefruit slice.

Enjoy your refreshing Paloma! This cocktail is known for its bright citrus flavors and is perfect for hot days. Adjust the sweetness and citrus intensity by varying the amount of grapefruit soda and lime juice according to your taste preferences.

Espresso Martini

Ingredients:

- 1 1/2 oz vodka
- 1 oz coffee liqueur (such as Kahlúa)
- 1 oz freshly brewed espresso (chilled)
- 1/2 oz simple syrup (optional, adjust to taste)
- Ice cubes

Instructions:

1. Brew a shot of espresso and let it cool completely (you can speed up the cooling process by placing it in the fridge).
2. Fill a cocktail shaker with ice cubes.
3. Add vodka, coffee liqueur, chilled espresso, and simple syrup (if using) to the shaker.
4. Shake vigorously until well chilled and frothy (about 10-15 seconds).
5. Strain the mixture into a chilled martini glass.

Enjoy your sophisticated Espresso Martini! This cocktail combines the rich flavors of coffee and vodka with a touch of sweetness from the coffee liqueur. Adjust the sweetness by varying the amount of simple syrup according to your preference. It's a perfect after-dinner drink or pick-me-up cocktail.

Mint Julep

Ingredients:

- 2 oz bourbon
- 1/2 oz simple syrup (or 1 teaspoon sugar)
- 8-10 fresh mint leaves, plus a sprig for garnish
- Crushed ice

Instructions:

1. In a Julep cup or a highball glass, muddle the mint leaves with the simple syrup (or sugar) to release the mint's essential oils. Be gentle to avoid tearing the mint leaves.
2. Fill the cup or glass with crushed ice.
3. Pour the bourbon over the ice.
4. Stir gently to mix and chill the drink.
5. Garnish with a sprig of mint.

Enjoy your classic Mint Julep! This cocktail is a staple of the Kentucky Derby and is known for its refreshing mint flavor combined with the smoothness of bourbon. Adjust the sweetness by varying the amount of simple syrup or sugar according to your taste preference.

Tom Collins

Ingredients:

- 2 oz gin
- 1 oz fresh lemon juice
- 1/2 oz simple syrup
- Club soda
- Lemon wheel and cherry for garnish
- Ice cubes

Instructions:

1. Fill a cocktail shaker with ice cubes.
2. Add gin, fresh lemon juice, and simple syrup to the shaker.
3. Shake well until chilled.
4. Strain the mixture into a Collins glass filled with ice cubes.
5. Top off with club soda.
6. Garnish with a lemon wheel and a cherry.

Enjoy your classic Tom Collins! This cocktail is light and citrusy, making it a perfect choice for a refreshing drink. Adjust the sweetness by varying the amount of simple syrup according to your taste preferences.

French 75

Ingredients:

- 1 oz gin
- 1/2 oz fresh lemon juice
- 1/2 oz simple syrup
- 3 oz Champagne or sparkling wine
- Lemon twist for garnish
- Ice cubes

Instructions:

1. Fill a cocktail shaker with ice cubes.
2. Add gin, fresh lemon juice, and simple syrup to the shaker.
3. Shake well until chilled.
4. Strain the mixture into a chilled champagne flute or coupe glass.
5. Top off with Champagne or sparkling wine.
6. Garnish with a lemon twist.

Enjoy your elegant French 75! This cocktail is perfect for celebrations, combining the bright citrus flavors of lemon with the effervescence of Champagne and the botanical notes of gin. Adjust the sweetness by varying the amount of simple syrup according to your taste preferences.

Sidecar

Ingredients:

- 2 oz cognac or brandy
- 1 oz triple sec (such as Cointreau)
- 3/4 oz fresh lemon juice
- Lemon twist or orange twist for garnish
- Superfine sugar for rimming (optional)
- Ice cubes

Instructions:

1. If rimming the glass with sugar, moisten the rim with a lemon wedge and dip it into superfine sugar. Let it dry for a moment.
2. Fill a cocktail shaker with ice cubes.
3. Add cognac (or brandy), triple sec, and fresh lemon juice to the shaker.
4. Shake well until chilled.
5. Strain the mixture into a chilled cocktail glass (coupe or martini glass).
6. Garnish with a lemon twist or orange twist.

Enjoy your classic Sidecar! This cocktail is known for its harmonious blend of tartness from the lemon juice, sweetness from the triple sec, and the rich flavor of cognac or brandy. Adjust the sweetness and tartness by varying the amount of lemon juice and triple sec according to your taste preferences.

Blue Lagoon

Ingredients:

- 1 1/2 oz vodka
- 1 oz blue curaçao
- Lemonade (or lemon-lime soda)
- Lemon wheel or cherry for garnish
- Ice cubes

Instructions:

1. Fill a highball glass with ice cubes.
2. Pour in the vodka and blue curaçao.
3. Top up with lemonade (or lemon-lime soda) to fill the glass.
4. Stir gently to combine.
5. Garnish with a lemon wheel or cherry.

Enjoy your refreshing Blue Lagoon! This cocktail is perfect for summer, with its bright color and citrusy flavor. Adjust the sweetness by choosing between lemonade and lemon-lime soda, and varying the proportions according to your taste preferences.

White Russian

Ingredients:

- 2 oz vodka
- 1 oz coffee liqueur (such as Kahlúa)
- 1 oz heavy cream or milk
- Ice cubes

Instructions:

1. Fill a rocks glass with ice cubes.
2. Pour in the vodka and coffee liqueur.
3. Float the heavy cream or milk on top by slowly pouring it over the back of a spoon.
4. Stir gently if desired.

Enjoy your classic White Russian! This cocktail combines the smoothness of vodka with the rich flavors of coffee liqueur and cream, making it a perfect after-dinner drink. Adjust the creaminess by using more or less cream or milk according to your preference.

Gimlet

Ingredients:

- 2 oz gin
- 3/4 oz fresh lime juice
- 3/4 oz simple syrup
- Lime wheel for garnish
- Ice cubes

Instructions:

1. Fill a cocktail shaker with ice cubes.
2. Add gin, fresh lime juice, and simple syrup to the shaker.
3. Shake well until chilled.
4. Strain the mixture into a chilled cocktail glass.
5. Garnish with a lime wheel.

Enjoy your classic Gimlet! This cocktail is known for its crisp and refreshing flavor, perfectly balancing the botanicals of gin with the tartness of lime and the sweetness of simple syrup. Adjust the sweetness and tartness by varying the amount of simple syrup and lime juice according to your taste preferences.

Caipirinha

Ingredients:

- 2 oz cachaça
- 1 lime, cut into wedges
- 2 teaspoons sugar
- Ice cubes

Instructions:

1. Place the lime wedges in a glass (preferably a rocks glass).
2. Add the sugar on top of the lime wedges.
3. Muddle the lime and sugar together to release the lime juice and dissolve the sugar.
4. Fill the glass with ice cubes.
5. Pour the cachaça over the ice.
6. Stir well to mix the ingredients.

Enjoy your classic Caipirinha! This cocktail is known for its refreshing and tangy flavor, perfectly balancing the sweetness of the sugar with the tartness of the lime and the unique taste of cachaça. Adjust the sweetness by varying the amount of sugar according to your preference.

Bellini

Ingredients:

- 2 oz peach purée (or peach nectar)
- 4 oz Prosecco (or any sparkling wine)
- Peach slice for garnish (optional)
- Ice cubes (optional, if using peach nectar)

Instructions:

1. If using peach purée, ensure it is chilled. If using peach nectar, you can chill it with ice cubes.
2. Pour the peach purée (or peach nectar) into a champagne flute.
3. Slowly top up with chilled Prosecco.
4. Stir gently to combine.
5. Garnish with a peach slice, if desired.

Enjoy your classic Bellini! This cocktail is known for its light, fruity flavor, perfect for brunches and celebrations. Adjust the proportions of peach purée and Prosecco according to your taste preferences.

Sazerac

Ingredients:

- 2 oz rye whiskey (or cognac)
- 1 sugar cube (or 1/2 oz simple syrup)
- 2-3 dashes Peychaud's bitters
- Absinthe (for rinsing the glass)
- Lemon peel for garnish
- Ice cubes

Instructions:

1. Chill an Old Fashioned glass by filling it with ice water. Let it sit while you prepare the cocktail.
2. In a mixing glass, muddle the sugar cube with a few dashes of Peychaud's bitters. If using simple syrup, combine it with the bitters.
3. Add the rye whiskey (or cognac) to the mixing glass and fill with ice cubes. Stir well until chilled.
4. Discard the ice water from the Old Fashioned glass. Add a small amount of absinthe to the glass and swirl it around to coat the inside. Discard any excess absinthe.
5. Strain the chilled whiskey mixture into the absinthe-rinsed glass.
6. Twist the lemon peel over the drink to express its oils, then rub it around the rim of the glass. Drop the peel into the drink or discard it.

Enjoy your classic Sazerac! This cocktail is known for its strong, aromatic flavors, with the anise notes from the absinthe complementing the spiciness of the rye whiskey and the sweetness of the sugar. Adjust the amount of absinthe and sugar to suit your taste preferences.

Piña Colada

Ingredients:

- 2 oz white rum
- 3 oz pineapple juice
- 1 oz coconut cream
- 1 oz heavy cream (optional, for a creamier texture)
- 1/2 oz simple syrup (optional, adjust to taste)
- Pineapple slice and maraschino cherry for garnish
- Ice cubes

Instructions:

1. In a blender, combine white rum, pineapple juice, coconut cream, heavy cream (if using), and simple syrup (if using).
2. Add a handful of ice cubes.
3. Blend until smooth and creamy.
4. Pour into a chilled hurricane glass or any tall glass.
5. Garnish with a pineapple slice and maraschino cherry.

Enjoy your classic Piña Colada! This cocktail is perfect for relaxing by the beach or poolside, with its creamy coconut and sweet pineapple flavors. Adjust the sweetness and creaminess by varying the amount of simple syrup and heavy cream according to your taste preferences.

Irish Coffee

Ingredients:

- 1 1/2 oz Irish whiskey
- 1 cup hot brewed coffee
- 1-2 teaspoons brown sugar (adjust to taste)
- Heavy cream, lightly whipped
- Ground nutmeg or cocoa powder (optional, for garnish)

Instructions:

1. Start by preheating a heat-resistant glass or mug by filling it with hot water. Let it sit for a minute, then discard the water.
2. Pour hot brewed coffee into the preheated glass or mug until it's about 3/4 full.
3. Stir in the brown sugar until it dissolves.
4. Add Irish whiskey and stir gently to combine.
5. Carefully float the lightly whipped heavy cream on top of the coffee by pouring it over the back of a spoon. The cream should sit on top without mixing into the coffee.
6. Optionally, dust with ground nutmeg or cocoa powder for garnish.

Enjoy your classic Irish Coffee! This cocktail combines the rich flavors of Irish whiskey with the smoothness of coffee and the creaminess of whipped cream, creating a comforting and indulgent drink. Adjust the sweetness by varying the amount of brown sugar according to your taste preferences.

Tequila Sunrise

Ingredients:

- 2 oz tequila (preferably silver or blanco)
- 4 oz orange juice
- 1/2 oz grenadine syrup
- Orange slice and cherry for garnish
- Ice cubes

Instructions:

1. Fill a highball glass with ice cubes.
2. Pour in the tequila and orange juice.
3. Stir gently to mix.
4. Slowly pour the grenadine syrup over the back of a spoon to create a gradient effect (the syrup should sink to the bottom).
5. Garnish with an orange slice and cherry.

Enjoy your vibrant Tequila Sunrise! This cocktail is perfect for brunch or relaxing by the pool, with its sweet and fruity flavors complementing the tequila. Adjust the sweetness by varying the amount of grenadine syrup according to your taste preferences.

Aperol Spritz

Ingredients:

- 2 oz Aperol
- 3 oz Prosecco (or any sparkling wine)
- Splash of soda water
- Orange slice for garnish
- Ice cubes

Instructions:

1. Fill a wine glass or large balloon glass with ice cubes.
2. Add Aperol to the glass.
3. Top up with Prosecco.
4. Add a splash of soda water.
5. Stir gently to mix.
6. Garnish with an orange slice.

Enjoy your classic Aperol Spritz! This cocktail is known for its bright orange color, bittersweet flavor, and refreshing effervescence. It's perfect for sipping before dinner as an aperitif. Adjust the proportions of Aperol and Prosecco according to your taste preferences, but the typical ratio is 2 parts Aperol to 3 parts Prosecco.

Long Island Iced Tea

Ingredients:

- 1/2 oz vodka
- 1/2 oz white rum
- 1/2 oz gin
- 1/2 oz tequila
- 1/2 oz triple sec (orange liqueur)
- 1 oz fresh lemon juice
- 1/2 oz simple syrup
- Cola (to top)
- Lemon wedge for garnish
- Ice cubes

Instructions:

1. Fill a cocktail shaker with ice cubes.
2. Add vodka, white rum, gin, tequila, triple sec, fresh lemon juice, and simple syrup to the shaker.
3. Shake well until chilled.
4. Strain the mixture into a highball glass filled with ice cubes.
5. Top off with cola to taste.
6. Garnish with a lemon wedge.

Enjoy your Long Island Iced Tea! This cocktail packs a punch with its mix of spirits and citrus flavors, balanced by the sweetness of cola. Be cautious, as it's stronger than it tastes due to the combination of liquors. Adjust the sweetness by varying the amount of simple syrup and cola according to your taste preferences.

Mojito

Ingredients:

- 2 oz white rum
- 1 oz fresh lime juice (approximately juice of 1 lime)
- 2 teaspoons white sugar (adjust to taste)
- 6-8 fresh mint leaves
- Club soda
- Ice cubes

Instructions:

1. In a sturdy glass or cocktail shaker, muddle the fresh mint leaves with the sugar and lime juice. Muddle gently to release the mint oils, but avoid tearing the leaves.
2. Fill the glass with ice cubes.
3. Pour in the white rum.
4. Stir well to mix the ingredients.
5. Top off with club soda to taste.
6. Garnish with a sprig of fresh mint and a lime wedge.

Enjoy your classic Mojito! This cocktail is known for its crisp and refreshing flavor, with the mint complementing the citrusy lime and the kick of rum. Adjust the sweetness and strength by varying the amount of sugar and rum according to your preference.

Margarita

Ingredients:

- 2 oz tequila (preferably silver or blanco)
- 1 oz triple sec (such as Cointreau or Grand Marnier)
- 3/4 oz fresh lime juice
- 1/2 oz simple syrup (optional, adjust to taste)
- Salt for rimming (optional)
- Lime wheel or wedge for garnish
- Ice cubes

Instructions:

1. If rimming the glass with salt, moisten the rim with a lime wedge and dip it into salt.
2. Fill a cocktail shaker with ice cubes.
3. Add tequila, triple sec, fresh lime juice, and simple syrup (if using) to the shaker.
4. Shake well until chilled.
5. Strain the mixture into a rocks glass filled with ice cubes.
6. Garnish with a lime wheel or wedge.

Enjoy your classic Margarita! This cocktail is known for its perfect balance of tequila, citrusy lime juice, and orange liqueur, with optional sweetness from simple syrup. Adjust the sweetness by varying the amount of simple syrup according to your taste preferences. It's perfect for enjoying on its own or paired with Mexican cuisine.

Daiquiri

Ingredients:

- 2 oz white rum
- 3/4 oz fresh lime juice
- 1/2 oz simple syrup
- Lime wheel or wedge for garnish
- Ice cubes

Instructions:

1. Fill a cocktail shaker with ice cubes.
2. Add white rum, fresh lime juice, and simple syrup to the shaker.
3. Shake well until chilled.
4. Strain the mixture into a chilled cocktail glass (coupe or martini glass).
5. Garnish with a lime wheel or wedge.

Enjoy your classic Daiquiri! This cocktail is known for its crisp and citrusy flavor, with the sweetness of the simple syrup balancing the tartness of the lime juice and the smoothness of the rum. Adjust the sweetness by varying the amount of simple syrup according to your taste preferences. It's perfect for sipping on a warm day or as a refreshing aperitif.

Manhattan

Ingredients:

- 2 oz rye whiskey (or bourbon)
- 1 oz sweet vermouth
- 2 dashes Angostura bitters
- Maraschino cherry for garnish
- Ice cubes

Instructions:

1. Fill a mixing glass or cocktail shaker with ice cubes.
2. Add rye whiskey (or bourbon), sweet vermouth, and Angostura bitters to the mixing glass.
3. Stir well until chilled and properly diluted, about 30 seconds.
4. Strain the mixture into a chilled cocktail glass (preferably a coupe or martini glass).
5. Garnish with a maraschino cherry.

Enjoy your classic Manhattan! This cocktail is known for its smooth and complex flavors, with the spicy rye whiskey or bourbon balanced by the sweetness of the vermouth and the aromatic complexity of the bitters. Adjust the ratio of whiskey to vermouth according to your taste preferences—some prefer a slightly drier or sweeter Manhattan.

Old Fashioned

Ingredients:

- 2 oz whiskey or bourbon
- 1 sugar cube (or 1/2 oz simple syrup)
- 2-3 dashes Angostura bitters
- Orange peel
- Ice cubes

Instructions:

1. Place the sugar cube in an Old Fashioned glass (or a rocks glass).
2. Add 2-3 dashes of Angostura bitters directly onto the sugar cube.
3. Muddle the sugar cube and bitters together to dissolve the sugar.
4. Add a few ice cubes to the glass.
5. Pour the whiskey or bourbon over the ice and stir well to combine.
6. Twist the orange peel over the drink to release its oils, then rub it around the rim of the glass. Drop the peel into the drink or discard it.

Enjoy your classic Old Fashioned! This cocktail is appreciated for its simplicity and depth of flavor, with the whiskey or bourbon taking center stage and the bitters adding complexity. Adjust the sweetness by varying the amount of sugar or simple syrup according to your taste preferences.

Negroni

Ingredients:

- 1 oz gin
- 1 oz Campari
- 1 oz sweet vermouth
- Orange twist or slice for garnish
- Ice cubes

Instructions:

1. Fill a mixing glass or cocktail shaker with ice cubes.
2. Add gin, Campari, and sweet vermouth to the mixing glass.
3. Stir well until chilled and properly diluted, about 30 seconds.
4. Strain the mixture into a rocks glass filled with ice cubes.
5. Garnish with an orange twist or slice.

Enjoy your classic Negroni! This cocktail is characterized by its bitter and herbal notes from the Campari, balanced by the sweetness of the vermouth and the botanicals of the gin. The orange garnish adds a citrusy aroma that complements the drink perfectly. Adjust the ratio of ingredients according to your taste preferences—some prefer a slightly more or less bitter profile by adjusting the Campari or vermouth.

Whiskey Sour

Ingredients:

- 2 oz whiskey (bourbon or rye)
- 3/4 oz fresh lemon juice
- 1/2 oz simple syrup (adjust to taste)
- Lemon wheel or cherry for garnish
- Ice cubes

Instructions:

1. Fill a cocktail shaker with ice cubes.
2. Add whiskey, fresh lemon juice, and simple syrup to the shaker.
3. Shake well until chilled.
4. Strain the mixture into a rocks glass filled with ice cubes.
5. Garnish with a lemon wheel or cherry.

Enjoy your classic Whiskey Sour! This cocktail is loved for its refreshing tartness and smooth whiskey flavor, with the simple syrup balancing the acidity of the lemon juice. Adjust the sweetness by varying the amount of simple syrup according to your taste preferences. It's a perfect choice for both casual gatherings and more formal occasions.

Mai Tai

Ingredients:

- 2 oz aged rum
- 3/4 oz fresh lime juice
- 1/2 oz orange curaçao
- 1/4 oz orgeat syrup
- 1/4 oz simple syrup
- Mint sprig and lime wheel for garnish
- Crushed ice

Instructions:

1. Fill a cocktail shaker with crushed ice.
2. Add aged rum, fresh lime juice, orange curaçao, orgeat syrup, and simple syrup to the shaker.
3. Shake well until chilled.
4. Fill a rocks glass or tiki mug with crushed ice.
5. Strain the cocktail mixture into the glass or mug over the crushed ice.
6. Garnish with a mint sprig and lime wheel.

Enjoy your classic Mai Tai! This cocktail is known for its complex flavors, with the rum providing a rich base complemented by the citrusy notes of lime juice and the sweetness of curaçao and orgeat syrup. Adjust the sweetness by varying the amount of simple syrup or orgeat syrup according to your taste preferences. It's perfect for transporting you to a tropical paradise with every sip.

Moscow Mule

Ingredients:

- 2 oz vodka
- 1/2 oz fresh lime juice
- 4-6 oz ginger beer
- Lime wedge for garnish
- Ice cubes

Instructions:

1. Fill a copper mug (or highball glass) with ice cubes.
2. Pour vodka and fresh lime juice over the ice.
3. Top off with ginger beer, leaving a little space at the top.
4. Stir gently to mix.
5. Garnish with a lime wedge.

Enjoy your Moscow Mule! This cocktail is known for its crisp and spicy ginger flavor, balanced by the citrusy tartness of lime and the smoothness of vodka. The copper mug helps keep the drink cool and enhances the drinking experience. Adjust the ratio of vodka to ginger beer according to your taste preferences—some prefer a stronger kick of vodka, while others enjoy more ginger beer for a spicier taste.

Bloody Mary

Ingredients:

- 1 1/2 oz vodka
- 3 oz tomato juice
- 1/2 oz fresh lemon juice
- 2 dashes Worcestershire sauce
- 2 dashes hot sauce (such as Tabasco)
- Pinch of salt and black pepper
- Celery salt (optional, for rimming)
- Celery stalk, lemon wedge, and/or olives for garnish
- Ice cubes

Instructions:

1. If rimming the glass with celery salt, moisten the rim with a lemon wedge and dip it into celery salt.
2. Fill a highball glass with ice cubes.
3. Add vodka, tomato juice, fresh lemon juice, Worcestershire sauce, hot sauce, salt, and black pepper to the glass.
4. Stir well to mix all ingredients together.
5. Garnish with a celery stalk, lemon wedge, and/or olives.

Enjoy your classic Bloody Mary! This cocktail is known for its robust and savory flavors, with the vodka providing a neutral base for the tangy tomato juice and spicy seasonings. Adjust the level of spiciness by varying the amount of hot sauce according to your preference. It's perfect for brunch or as a refreshing pick-me-up any time of the day.

Paloma

Ingredients:

- 2 oz tequila (preferably blanco or silver)
- 1/2 oz fresh lime juice
- Pinch of salt (optional)
- Grapefruit soda (such as Jarritos or Squirt)
- Lime wedge for garnish
- Ice cubes

Instructions:

1. Fill a highball glass with ice cubes.
2. Add tequila and fresh lime juice to the glass.
3. Add a pinch of salt (optional).
4. Top off with grapefruit soda, leaving room to stir.
5. Stir gently to mix all ingredients together.
6. Garnish with a lime wedge.

Enjoy your classic Paloma! This cocktail is known for its crisp and citrusy flavors, with the tequila providing a subtle earthy undertone and the grapefruit soda adding a refreshing fizz. Adjust the sweetness and tartness by varying the amount of lime juice and soda according to your taste preferences. It's perfect for warm weather and pairs well with Mexican cuisine.

Tom Collins

Ingredients:

- 2 oz gin
- 1 oz fresh lemon juice
- 1/2 oz simple syrup
- Club soda
- Lemon wheel or cherry for garnish
- Ice cubes

Instructions:

1. Fill a Collins glass (or a tall glass) with ice cubes.
2. Add gin, fresh lemon juice, and simple syrup to the glass.
3. Stir well to mix the ingredients.
4. Top off with club soda, leaving a little space at the top.
5. Stir gently again to combine.
6. Garnish with a lemon wheel or cherry.

Enjoy your classic Tom Collins! This cocktail is known for its crisp and citrusy flavors, with the gin providing a botanical base complemented by the tartness of lemon juice and the sweetness of simple syrup. Adjust the sweetness by varying the amount of simple syrup according to your taste preferences. It's perfect for a refreshing drink on a warm day or as a pre-dinner cocktail.

Mint Julep

Ingredients:

- 2 oz bourbon
- 1/2 oz simple syrup
- 3-4 fresh mint leaves, plus extra for garnish
- Crushed ice

Instructions:

1. In a julep cup or old-fashioned glass, muddle the mint leaves and simple syrup together gently to release the mint oils.
2. Fill the glass with crushed ice.
3. Pour bourbon over the ice.
4. Stir gently to mix and chill the drink.
5. Top with more crushed ice if needed.
6. Garnish with a mint sprig.

Enjoy your classic Mint Julep! This cocktail is known for its smooth bourbon flavor combined with the refreshing mint and sweetness from the simple syrup. The crushed ice helps to keep the drink cold and refreshing. Adjust the sweetness by varying the amount of simple syrup according to your taste preferences. It's a perfect choice for a hot summer day or any time you want to enjoy a taste of Southern hospitality.

Cosmopolitan

Ingredients:

- 1 1/2 oz vodka
- 1 oz triple sec (such as Cointreau)
- 1/2 oz fresh lime juice
- 1/2 oz cranberry juice
- Orange twist or lime wedge for garnish
- Ice cubes

Instructions:

1. Fill a cocktail shaker with ice cubes.
2. Add vodka, triple sec, fresh lime juice, and cranberry juice to the shaker.
3. Shake well until chilled.
4. Strain the mixture into a chilled martini glass.
5. Garnish with an orange twist or lime wedge.

Enjoy your classic Cosmopolitan! This cocktail is known for its balanced blend of vodka, citrusy lime juice, and the tartness of cranberry juice. Adjust the sweetness by varying the amount of cranberry juice or adding a splash of simple syrup if desired. It's perfect for both casual gatherings and elegant occasions, with its vibrant pink hue and refreshing taste.

Piña Colada

Ingredients:

- 2 oz white rum
- 2 oz coconut cream
- 2 oz pineapple juice
- 1/2 oz fresh lime juice
- Pineapple slice and maraschino cherry for garnish
- Ice cubes

Instructions:

1. In a blender, combine white rum, coconut cream, pineapple juice, and fresh lime juice.
2. Add a handful of ice cubes.
3. Blend until smooth and creamy.
4. Pour into a chilled hurricane glass or any tall glass.
5. Garnish with a pineapple slice and maraschino cherry.

Enjoy your classic Piña Colada! This cocktail is famous for its tropical flavors, with the rum providing a slight kick, the coconut cream adding richness, and the pineapple juice offering sweetness and tanginess. Adjust the sweetness by varying the amount of coconut cream or pineapple juice according to your taste preferences. It's perfect for sipping by the pool or at a beachside bar, bringing a taste of the tropics wherever you are.

Martini

Ingredients:

- 2 oz gin or vodka (you can choose your preference)
- 1/2 oz dry vermouth
- Lemon twist or olive for garnish
- Ice cubes

Instructions:

1. Fill a mixing glass or cocktail shaker with ice cubes.
2. Add gin or vodka and dry vermouth to the mixing glass.
3. Stir or shake well (stirring is traditional for a smoother texture, shaking adds more dilution and chill).
4. Strain the mixture into a chilled martini glass.
5. Garnish with a lemon twist or olive.

Enjoy your classic Martini! The choice between gin or vodka and the ratio of vermouth to spirit can vary based on personal preference. A traditional Martini tends to be dry, with less vermouth, while a wet Martini has more vermouth. Experiment to find the balance you prefer. It's a cocktail that's perfect for sophisticated occasions or quiet evenings.

Caipirinha

Ingredients:

- 2 oz cachaça (Brazilian sugarcane spirit)
- 1/2 lime, cut into wedges
- 2 teaspoons granulated sugar (adjust to taste)
- Ice cubes

Instructions:

1. Place lime wedges and granulated sugar in an Old Fashioned glass or rocks glass.
2. Muddle the lime and sugar together to release the lime juice and dissolve the sugar.
3. Fill the glass with ice cubes.
4. Pour cachaça over the ice and stir well to mix.
5. Garnish with a lime wedge.

Enjoy your classic Caipirinha! This cocktail is known for its vibrant lime flavor, with the cachaça providing a distinct and slightly sweet undertone. Adjust the sweetness by varying the amount of sugar according to your taste preferences. It's perfect for sipping on a warm day or pairing with Brazilian cuisine.

French 75

Ingredients:

- 1 oz gin
- 1/2 oz fresh lemon juice
- 1/2 oz simple syrup (1:1 ratio of water to sugar)
- Champagne or sparkling wine
- Lemon twist or cherry for garnish
- Ice cubes

Instructions:

1. Fill a cocktail shaker with ice cubes.
2. Add gin, fresh lemon juice, and simple syrup to the shaker.
3. Shake well until chilled.
4. Strain the mixture into a champagne flute or coupe glass.
5. Top with champagne or sparkling wine.
6. Garnish with a lemon twist or cherry.

Enjoy your classic French 75! This cocktail is known for its bubbly and citrusy flavors, with the gin providing a botanical base complemented by the tartness of lemon juice and the sweetness of simple syrup. Adjust the sweetness by varying the amount of simple syrup according to your taste preferences. It's perfect for celebrating special occasions or adding a touch of elegance to any gathering.

Sangria

Ingredients:

- 1 bottle (750 ml) red wine (such as Spanish rioja or any fruity red wine)
- 1/4 cup brandy or orange liqueur (such as Triple Sec)
- 1/4 cup orange juice
- 1/4 cup freshly squeezed lemon juice
- 2 tablespoons granulated sugar (adjust to taste)
- 1 orange, thinly sliced
- 1 lemon, thinly sliced
- 1 lime, thinly sliced
- 1 apple, cored and thinly sliced
- 1 cup club soda or lemon-lime soda (optional, for serving)
- Ice cubes

Instructions:

1. In a large pitcher, combine the red wine, brandy or orange liqueur, orange juice, lemon juice, and granulated sugar. Stir until the sugar dissolves.
2. Add the sliced orange, lemon, lime, and apple to the pitcher.
3. Refrigerate for at least 2 hours, or preferably overnight, to allow the flavors to meld.
4. Before serving, add ice cubes to individual glasses (if desired) and pour the Sangria over the ice.
5. Optionally, top each glass with a splash of club soda or lemon-lime soda for a bit of fizz.
6. Garnish each glass with a slice of orange, lemon, lime, or apple.

Enjoy your classic Sangria! This cocktail is known for its fruity and refreshing flavors, with the citrus juices adding brightness and the fruit slices adding a burst of color and flavor. Adjust the sweetness by varying the amount of sugar or adding more fruit juice if desired. It's perfect for serving at parties or enjoying on a sunny afternoon with friends.

www.ingramcontent.com/pod-product-compliance
Lightning Source LLC
LaVergne TN
LVHW081331060526
838201LV00055B/2575